# SUPER SEATWORK

Linguistic Exercises

by Mary Pecci

Copyright © 1990 Mary F. Pecci

All Rights Reserved

Permission is granted to reproduce
this material for classroom use.

**SECOND EDITION**

Additional copies may be ordered from:

PECCI EDUCATIONAL PUBLISHERS
440 Davis Court, No. 405
San Francisco, CA 94111

ISBN NO. 0-943220-03-3

These materials are derived from:

AT LAST! A READING METHOD FOR EVERY CHILD!

Written by: Mary F. Pecci, Reading Specialist
Edited by: Ernest F. Pecci, Child Psychiatrist

# Acknowledgements

Sincere appreciation is extended to the following teachers for their valuable suggestions and contributions and for allowing me to test these materials in their classrooms: Patricia Armanini, Dorothy Brus, Leonarda Brush, Laurel Manders, Diana Craft Olson and June Triesch - with a special thanks to Joy Abrams of Joyez Press, for making initial publications possible.

# Contents

| | | | |
|---|---|---|---|
| I | - | Short Vowel Families | p. 1 - 21 |
| II | - | Long Vowel Families (e - on - the - end) | p. 22 - 34 |
| III | - | Long Vowel Families (two vowels together) | p. 35 - 48 |
| IV | - | Sight Families | p. 49 - 59 |
| V | - | Summary Exercises | p. 60 - 65 |
| VI | - | Phonic Review Exercises | p. 66 - 106 |

# Introduction

English is a linguistic language because most words can not be sounded out letter-for-letter. They must be decoded by groups of letters, which we will call "Families". For example, you can't sound out the word "talk" letter-for-letter. It must be decoded as follows:

|  | Teacher: | Students: |
|---|---|---|
| t<u>alk</u> | What's the family? | alk |
|  | What's the word? | talk |

There are only <u>four</u> groups of families:

### 1. SHORT VOWEL FAMILIES:

<u>Rule</u>: If there's only one vowel, it's short.

|  | Teacher: | Students: |
|---|---|---|
| c<u>an</u> | What's the family? | an |
|  | What's the word? | can |

### 2. LONG VOWEL FAMILIES:

<u>Rule</u>: The "e" on the end makes the vowel long.

|  | Teacher: | Students: |
|---|---|---|
| c<u>ane</u> | What's the family? | ane |
|  | What's the word? | cane |

### 3. LONG VOWEL FAMILIES:

<u>Rule</u>: When two vowels go walking,
The first one does the talking.

|  | Teacher: | Students: |
|---|---|---|
| b<u>oat</u> | What's the family? | oat |
|  | What's the word? | boat |

### 4. SIGHT FAMILIES:

<u>Rule</u>: This is a Sight Family because you can't sound it out - you have to memorize it.

|  | Teacher: | Students: |
|---|---|---|
| n<u>ight</u> | What's the family? | ight |
|  | What's the word? | night |

These four groups of Families cover about 90% of words and they will greatly facilitate the handling of the remaining 10% of words, which are exceptions to these rules.

For comprehensive details on how to teach reading, order AT LAST! **A READING METHOD FOR EVERY CHILD!** This book presents a simple phonic technique which eliminates all of the nitty-gritty and tedium which causes failure. It was developed during 10 years of research and has proven successful with every possible type of reading disability - at Juvenile Court, in the ghettos, with all socio-economic groups, with the mentally retarded, English second language students and those who have been professionally diagnosed as having learning disability, neurological handicaps and dyslexia. Also included is a multitude of motivation and reinforcement techniques which have been collected over the years from master teachers.

## Books by Mary Pecci:

AT LAST!  A READING METHOD FOR EVERY CHILD!

SUPER SEATWORK - Content Areas
SUPER SEATWORK - Letter-Recognition
SUPER SEATWORK - Linguistic Exercises
SUPER SEATWORK - Word Skills
SUPER SEATWORK - Color Words
SUPER SEATWORK - Number Words
SUPER SEATWORK - Phonic Grab Bag

How To Discipline Your Class For Joyful Teaching!

# Short Vowel Family Exercises

**Rule:** If there's only one vowel, it's short.

The most effective way to develop mastery of these Families is to have each student actively involved in utilizing a number of learning modalities - seeing, hearing, writing and reciting. The teacher must dictate the initial consonant each time, while the children write the consonant and recite the word. This will also keep the pace moving smoothly and the message clear. Call on individual students at intervals to check attention and accuracy.

| Aa | | |
|---|---|---|
| at | an | ap |
| at | an | ap |
| at | an | ap |
| at | an | ap |

| Teacher: | Students: |
|---|---|
| Say "A - ahh - apple". | A - ahh - apple |
| Sound out the first family. | ahh-tt |
| Add a "c" - What's the word? | cat |
| Add a "b" - What's the word? | bat |
| Add an "h" - What's the word? | hat |
| Read that back. | at, cat, bat, hat |
| Sound out the next family, etc. | |

**Completed Sheet:**

| Aa | | |
|---|---|---|
| at | an | ap |
| cat | ran | map |
| bat | man | flap |
| hat | than | strap |

# Aa

| at at at at | an an an an | ap ap ap ap |

# Ee

et  et  et  et

en  en  en  en

ed  ed  ed  ed

# Ii

ip　ip　ip　ip

in　in　in　in

it　it　it　it

# o

_ot_
ot
ot
ot

_op_
op
op
op

_og_
og
og
og

# Uu

| ug | ug | ug | ug |

| un | un | un | un |

| ut | ut | ut | ut |

# Aa

ad
ad
ad

ag
ag
ag

ab
ab
ab

# Ee

ell ell ell ell

end end end end

eg eg eg eg

# Ii

ib ib ib ib

ig ig ig ig

id id id id

10

# Oo

| oss | oss | oss | oss |

| op | op | op | op |

| od | od | od | od |

# Uu

| up  | uff |
| up  | uff |
| up  | uff |

| ud  | uzz |
| ud  | uzz |
| ud  | uzz |

| ub  | uch |
| ub  | uch |
| ub  | uch |

| Uu 🌂 | ut | ut | ut | ut |
| Oo 🐙 | ot | ot | ot | ot |
| Ii | it | it | it | it |
| Ee | et | et | et | et |
| Aa 🍎 | at | at | at | at |

| | |
|---|---|
| Aa 🍎 | ack<br>ack<br>ack<br>ack |
| Ee 😀 | eck<br>eck<br>eck<br>eck |
| Ii 🐟 | ick<br>ick<br>ick<br>ick |
| Oo 🐙 | ock<br>ock<br>ock<br>ock |
| Uu ☂ | uck<br>uck<br>uck<br>uck |

| Aa 🍎 | ast | ast | ast | ast |
|---|---|---|---|---|
| Ee | est | est | est | est |
| Ii | ist | ist | ist | ist |
| Oo | ost | ost | ost | ost |
| Uu ☂ | ust | ust | ust | ust |

# Aa 🍎

and
and
and

# Ee

ent
ent
ent

# Oo

ond
ond
ond

| | |
|---|---|
| **Aa** 🍎 | ash ash ash ash |
| **Ii** 🐟 | ish ish ish ish |
| **Uu** ☂ | ush ush ush ush |

# Aa

## Let's Build Families

am
amp

an
and
ang
ank
ant
anch

Directions: Each time, add an initial consonant. It is very good practice for blending sounds.

# Ee

### Let's Build Families

| ell | ess | ep  | en   |
|-----|-----|-----|------|
| eld | esk | ept | end  |
| elp | est |     | ent  |
| elt |     |     | ench |

# Ii

## Let's Build Families

| | |
|---|---|
| in | |
| imp | |

| | |
|---|---|
| ill | |
| ilk | |
| ilt | |

| | |
|---|---|
| in | |
| ing | |
| ink | |
| int | |
| inch | |

| | |
|---|---|
| iss | |
| isk | |
| ist | |

# Oo

## Let's Build Families

on
ond
ong
onk

oss
ost

om
omp

# Uu

## Let's Build Families

| _um | _ull | _us | _un |
| _ump | _ulk | _usk | _und |
| | | _ust | _ung |
| | | | _unk |
| | | | _unt |
| | | | _unch |

# Long Vowel Family Exercises

**Rule:** The "e" on the end makes the vowel long.

The most effective way to develop mastery of these Families is to have each student actively involved in utilizing a number of learning modalities - seeing, hearing, writing and reciting. The teacher must dictate the initial consonant each time, while the children write the consonant and recite the word. This will also keep the pace moving smoothly and the message clear. Call on individual students at intervals to check attention and accuracy.

## Long A

| ade | ake | ape |
|-----|-----|-----|
| ade | ake | ape |
| ade | ake | ape |
| ade | ake | ape |

| Teacher: | Students: |
|---|---|
| Say "A says A". | A says A |
| Sound out the first family. | ade |
| Add an "m" - What's the word? | made |
| Add "sh"   - What's the word? | shade |
| Add "bl"   - What's the word? | blade |
| Read that back. | ade, made, shade, blade |
| Sound out the next family, etc. | |

### Completed Sheet:

**Long A**

| ade | ake | ape |
|------|------|-------|
| made | bake | cape |
| shade | cake | shape |
| blade | take | tape |

NOTE: For additional reinforcement, have the students make an arrow on the top family of each row from the "e" on the end to the vowel.

# Long A

ade ade ade ade

ake ake ake ake

ape ape ape ape

# Long A

| ane | ame | ale | age |
|-----|-----|-----|-----|
| ane | ame | ale | age |
| ane | ame | ale | age |
| ane | ame | ale | age |

# Long A

are
are  are  are

ace
ace  ace  ace

ase
ase  ase  ase

NOTE: Although the vowel doesn't have its true long sound when followed by an "r" (are, care), simplify the decoding process by giving it its true long sound. Once the word is known, the students automatically transfer the pronunciation into their own particular accent.

# Long A

| ate | ave | aze |
|---|---|---|
| ate | ave | aze |
| ate | ave | aze |
| ate | ave | aze |

# Long E

here
Pete
Gene

Steve
Zeke
theme

NOTE: There are not many families that can be made with long "e." However, the above exercises will acquaint the students with these combinations so they may handle them easily _within_ words.

# Long I

| ide | ike | ile |
|---|---|---|
| ide | ike | ile |
| ide | ike | ile |
| ide | ike | ile |

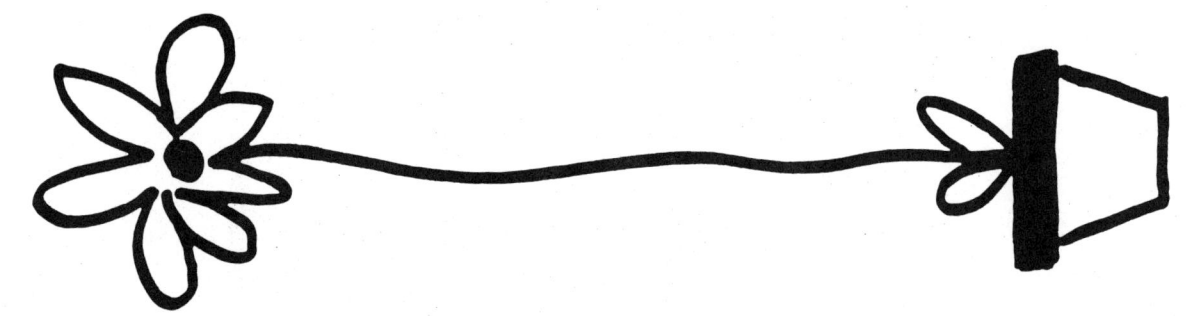

# Long I

| ive | ite | ire |
|---|---|---|
| ive | ite | ire |
| ive | ite | ire |
| ive | ite | ire |

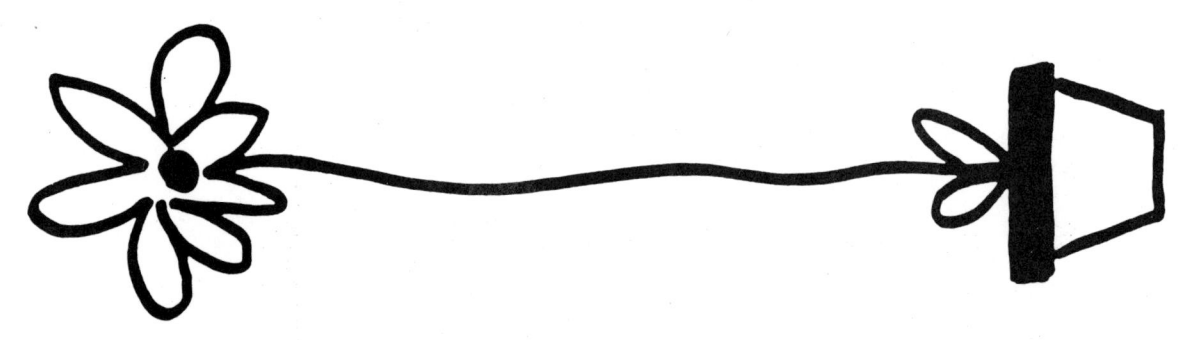

# Long O

| _ode | _oke | _ole |
| ode | oke | ole |
| ode | oke | ole |

# Long O

| ope | ope | ope | ope |

| one | one | one | one |

| ome | ome | ome | ome |

# Long O

ore ore ore ore

ote ote ote ote

ove ove ove ove

oze oze oze

# Long U

h uge
c ube
f ume

m ule
p ure
c ute

NOTE: There are not many families that can be made with long "u." However, the above exercises will acquaint the students with these combinations so they may handle them easily within words.

# Long Vowel Family Exercises

**Rule:** When two vowels go walking,
The first one does the talking.

The most effective way to develop mastery of these Families is to have each student actively involved in utilizing a number of learning modalities - seeing, hearing, writing and reciting. The teacher must dictate the initial consonant each time, while the children write the consonant and recite the word. This will also keep the pace moving smoothly and the message clear. Call on individual students at intervals to check attention and accuracy.

|  | When two vowels go walking, The first one does the talking. | |
|---|---|---|
| ai | ee | oa |
| ain | eet | oat |
| ain | eet | oat |
| ain | eet | oat |

| Teacher: | Students: |
|---|---|
| Say "A says A". | A says A |
| Sound out the first family. | ai, ain |
| Add an "r" - What's the word? | rain |
| Add an "m" - What's the word? | main |
| Add a "tr" - What's the word? | train |
| Read that back. | ai, rain, main, train |
| Sound out the next family, etc. | |

**Completed Sheet:**

|  | When two vowels go walking, The first one does the talking. | |
|---|---|---|
| ai | ee | oa |
| rain | meet | boat |
| main | feet | coat |
| train | sweet | goat |

35

When two vowels go walking,
The first one does the talking.

| oa | ee | ai |
| --- | --- | --- |
| oat | eet | ain |
| oat | eet | ain |
| oat | eet | ain |

NOTE: For additional reinforcement, have the students make an arrow on the first family in each row from the first vowel to the consonant.

When two vowels go walking,
The first one does the talking.

ea
ead
ead

ie
ie
ie

oe
oe
oe

When two vowels go walking,
The first one does the talking.

| ea | ai | ue |
| ean | ail | ue |
| ean | ail | ue |
| ean | ail | ue |

When two vowels go walking,
The first one does the talking.

ee
eep
eep

ui
uit
uit

ie
ie
ie

When two vowels go walking,
The first one does the talking.

| ea | ue | oa |
| eat | ue | oad |
| eat | ue | oad |
| eat | ue | oad |

# Long A

| ai | | |
|---|---|---|
| aid | aid | aid |

| ai | | |
|---|---|---|
| ail | ail | ail |

| ai | | |
|---|---|---|
| ain | ain | ain |

| ai | | |
|---|---|---|
| air | air | air |

| ai | | |
|---|---|---|
| ait | ait | ait |

NOTE: Although the vowel doesn't have its true long sound when followed by an "r" (air, hair), simplify the decoding process by giving it its true long sound. Once the word is known, the students automatically transfer the pronunciation into their own particular accent.

# Long E

| ee | ee | ee | ee |
|---|---|---|---|
| eem | eel | eek | eed |
| eem | eel | eek | eed |
| eem | eel | eek | eed |

# Long E

ee
een
een
een

ee
eep
eep
eep

ee
eet
eet
eet

43

# Long E

| ea | ea | ea | ea |
|---|---|---|---|
| ead | eak | eal | eat |
| ead | eak | eal | eat |
| ead | eak | eal | eat |

# Long E

ea
eam
eam
eam

ea
ean
ean
ean

ea
eap
eap
eap

ea
ear
ear
ear

# Long O

| oa | oa | oa | oa |
|---|---|---|---|
| oad | oat | oak | oast |
| oad | oat | oak | oast |
| oad | oat | oak | oast |

# Long O

| oa | oa | oa | oa |
|---|---|---|---|
| oal | oam | oan | oap |
| oal | oam | oan | oaf |

| Long U | ui | uit | uit | uit |
| --- | --- | --- | --- | --- |
| | ue | ue | ue | ue |
| Long O | oe | oe | oe | oe |
| Long I | ie | ie | ie | ie |

# Sight Families

These are the only Families which must be memorized because there is no common rule.

Teach just the <u>one</u> sound for each Family, as given in the sample word below:

<u>Sight Family:</u>

| | | | | |
|---|---|---|---|---|
| ay | oo | ew | ar | oy |
| oi | ow | ou | ound | ight |
| igh | alk | er | ir | ur |
| all | eight | eigh | aw | au |
| aught | ought | ange | tion | sion |

<u>Sample Word:</u>

| | | | | |
|---|---|---|---|---|
| day | zoo | new | car | boy |
| oil | now | out | found | night |
| high | walk | her | sir | fur |
| ball | weight | weigh | saw | auto |
| caught | thought | range | station | mission |

When all of these Sight Families have been introduced, mimeograph the front and back of p. 51-52, as shown, on oaktag or colored construction paper and have each child cut out a set of Sight Family Cards for home study. Fasten with a rubber band.

# Sight Family Exercises

**Rule:** This is a Sight Family because you can't sound it out - you have to memorize it.

The most effective way to develop mastery of these Families is to have each student actively involved in utilizing a number of learning modalities - seeing, hearing, writing and reciting. The teacher must dictate the initial consonant each time, while the children write the consonant and recite the word. This will also keep the pace moving smoothly and the message clear. Call on individual students at intervals to check attention and accuracy.

| Sight | | |
|---|---|---|
| ow | ou | ound |
| ow | oud | ound |
| ow | oud | ound |
| ow | ouch | ound |

| Teacher: | Students: |
|---|---|
| What is this Sight family? | ow |
| Add a "c" - What's the word? | cow |
| Add an "n" - What's the word? | now |
| Add an "h" - What's the word? | how |
| Read that back. | ow, cow, now, how |
| What's the next family, etc. | |

**Completed Sheet:**

| Sight | | |
|---|---|---|
| ow | ou | ound |
| cow | loud | round |
| now | proud | found |
| how | couch | sound |

| ay | oo | ew | ar | oy |
|---|---|---|---|---|
| oi | ow | ou | ound | ight |
| igh | alk | er | ir | ur |
| all | aw | eight | eigh | au |
| aught | ought | ange | tion | sion |

| boy | car | new | zoo | day |
| night | found | out | now | oil |
| fur | sir | her | walk | high |
| auto | weigh | weight | saw | ball |
| mission | station | range | thought | caught |

# Sight

| ow | ou | ound |
|---|---|---|
| ow | ou | ound |
| ow | oud | ound |
| ow | oud | ound |
|   | ouch |   |

# Sight

| ay | ar | alk | all |
|----|----|-----|-----|
| ay | ar | alk | all |
| ay | ar | alk | all |
| ay | ar | alk | all |

# Sight

| oo | ew | oy | oi |
|----|----|----|----|
| oo | ew | oy | oil |
| oo | ew | oy | oin |
| oo | ew | oy | oist |

# Sight

| ur | ur | urn | urf |

| ir | ir | irn | irl |

| er | er | erd | erm |

# Sight

aw
aw
aw

au
aul
ault

aught
aught
aughter

# Sight

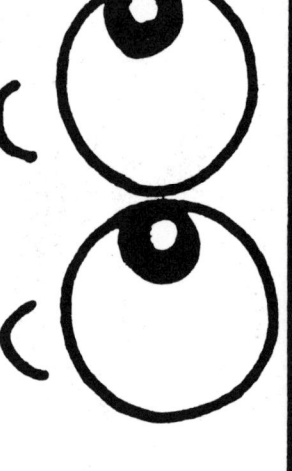

| eigh | eight | igh | ight |
|---|---|---|---|
| eigh | eight | igh | ight |
| eigh | eight | igh | ight |
| eigh | | igh | ight |

# Sight

| ought | ange | tion | sion |
|-------|------|------|------|
| ought | ange | station | mission |
| ought | ange | nation | pension |
| ought | ange | nation | tension |

# Summary Exercises

These Summary Exercises will bring the message in crystal clear and enable the children to quickly recognize any Family in words as they decode syllable by syllable.

The most effective way to develop mastery of these Families is to have each student actively involved in utilizing a number of learning modalities - seeing, hearing, writing and reciting. The teacher must dictate the initial consonant each time, while the children write the consonant and recite the word. This will also keep the pace moving smoothly and the message clear. Call on individual students at intervals to check attention and accuracy.

|  | A |
|---|---|
|  | at |
|  | ate |
|  | ait |
|  | alk |
|  |  |

| Teacher: | Students: |
|---|---|
| Why is the first family Short? | There's only one vowel. |
| Why is the next family Long? | There's an "e" on the end. |
| Why is the next family Long? | There are two vowels together. |
| Why is the last family Sight? | You can't sound it out. |

| Teacher: | Students: |
|---|---|
| What's the first family? | at |
| Add an "f" - What's the word? | fat |
| What's the next family? | ate |
| Add an "f" - What's the word? | fate |
| What's the next family? | ait |
| Add a "w" - What's the word? | wait |
| What's the last family? | alk |
| Add a "w" - What's the word? | walk |

Completed Sheet:

|  | A |
|---|---|
| f | at |
| f | ate |
| w | ait |
| w | alk |

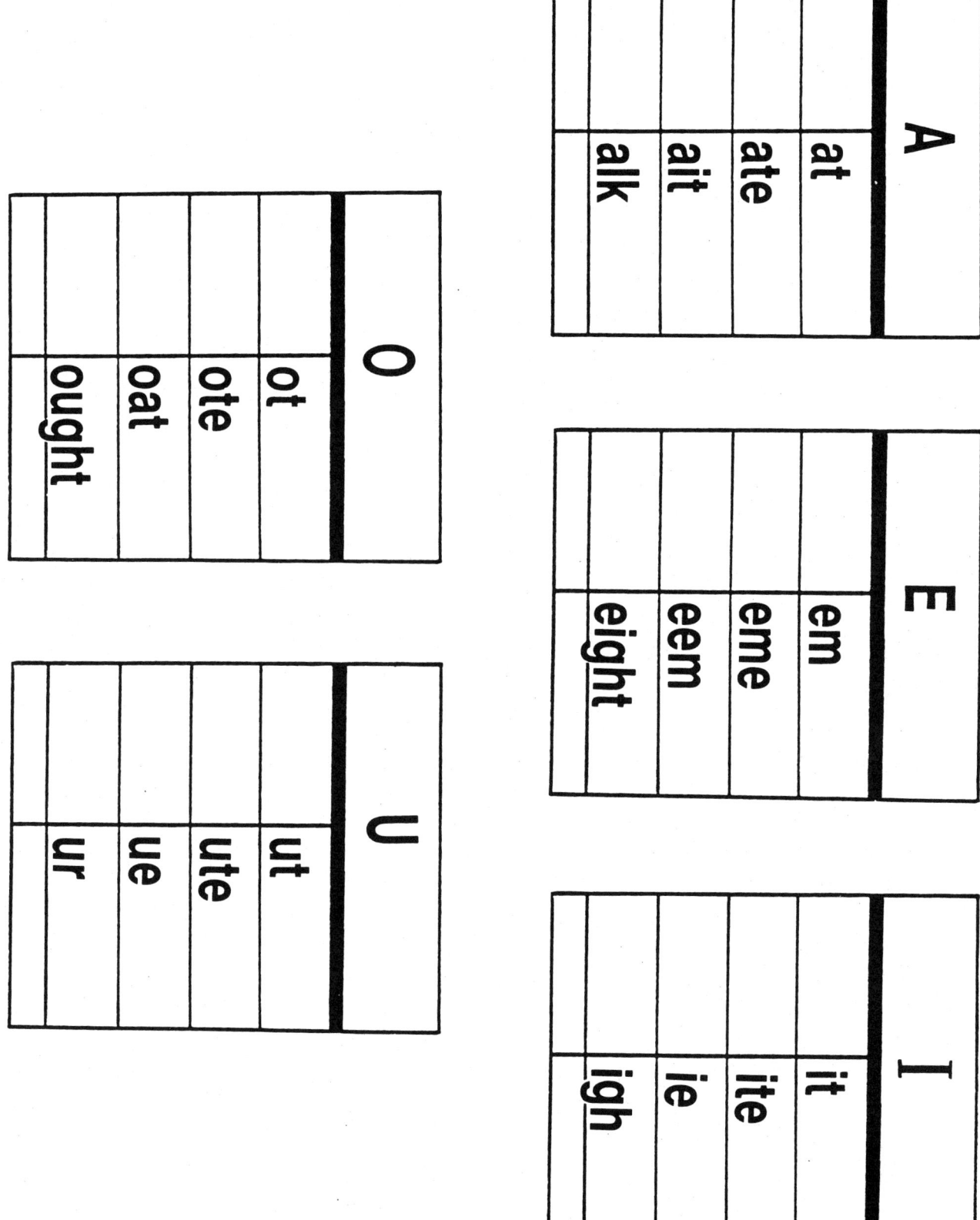

62

| A |  |  |  |  |  |
|---|---|---|---|---|---|
|  | an |  |  |  |  |
|  | ane |  |  |  |  |
|  | ain |  |  |  |  |
|  | aw |  |  |  |  |

| E |  |  |  |  |  |
|---|---|---|---|---|---|
|  | et |  |  |  |  |
|  | ete |  |  |  |  |
|  | eat |  |  |  |  |
|  | er |  |  |  |  |

| I |  |  |  |  |  |
|---|---|---|---|---|---|
|  | ip |  |  |  |  |
|  | ipe |  |  |  |  |
|  | ie |  |  |  |  |
|  | ir |  |  |  |  |

| O |  |  |  |  |  |
|---|---|---|---|---|---|
|  | op |  |  |  |  |
|  | ope |  |  |  |  |
|  | oap |  |  |  |  |
|  | ound |  |  |  |  |

| U |  |  |  |  |  |
|---|---|---|---|---|---|
|  | un |  |  |  |  |
|  | une |  |  |  |  |
|  | ue |  |  |  |  |
|  | ur |  |  |  |  |

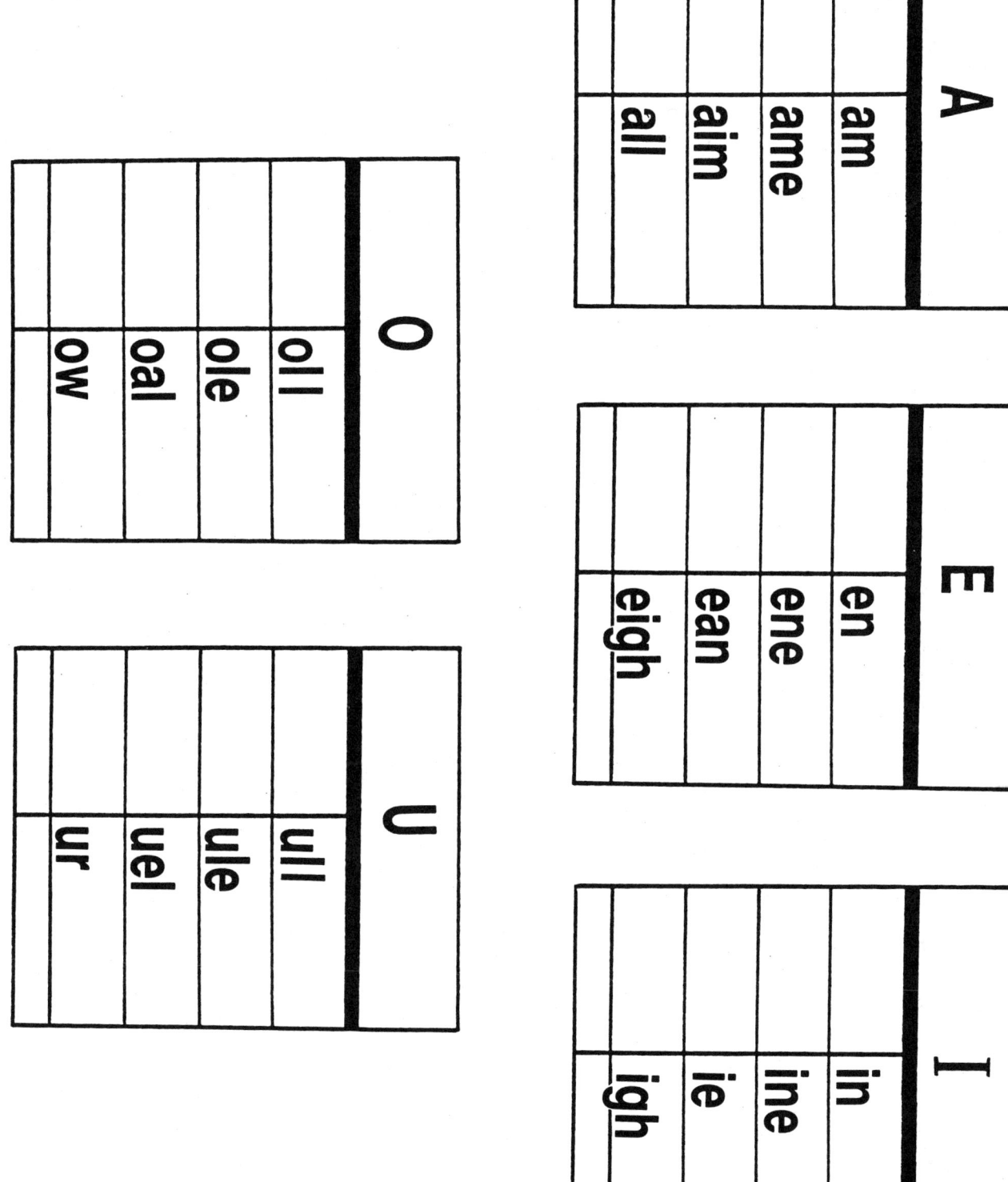

| A | | | | |
|---|---|---|---|---|
| am | ame | aim | all | |

| E | | | | |
|---|---|---|---|---|
| en | ene | ean | eigh | |

| I | | | | |
|---|---|---|---|---|
| in | ine | ie | igh | |

| O | | | | |
|---|---|---|---|---|
| oll | ole | oal | ow | |

| U | | | | |
|---|---|---|---|---|
| ull | ule | uel | ur | |

| A | | | | |
|---|---|---|---|---|
| | al | ale | ail | ar |
| | | | | |

| E | | | | |
|---|---|---|---|---|
| | et | ete | eet | er |
| | | | | |

| I | | | | |
|---|---|---|---|---|
| | im | ime | ie | ir |
| | | | | |

| O | | | | |
|---|---|---|---|---|
| | ock | oke | oak | oy |
| | | | | |

| U | | | | |
|---|---|---|---|---|
| | um | ume | ue | ur |
| | | | | |

| A |        |
|---|--------|
|   | ad     |
|   | ade    |
|   | aid    |
|   | ay     |

| E |        |
|---|--------|
|   | em     |
|   | eme    |
|   | eam    |
|   | ew     |

| I |        |
|---|--------|
|   | id     |
|   | ide    |
|   | ied    |
|   | igh    |

| O |        |
|---|--------|
|   | od     |
|   | ode    |
|   | oad    |
|   | oo     |

| U |        |
|---|--------|
|   | ub     |
|   | ube    |
|   | ue     |
|   | ur     |

# Phonic Review Exercises

The following exercises will strengthen the four groups of Linguistic Families and reinforce <u>Basic Phonics</u>, <u>Phonetic Spelling</u> and <u>Independent Decoding</u>. A completed sheet will resemble the following:

| Name: Fred | | | |
|---|---|---|---|
| Draw two pictures for each sound. | Write two words under each family. | | Draw the Mystery Picture. |
| c (cat picture) (cup picture) | at<br>cat<br>bat | en<br>ten<br>hen | top |
| fl (flag picture) (flower picture) | ow<br>now<br>how | ound<br>round<br>found | ball |

It is advisable to do one or two of these sheets with the children before assigning them for independent seatwork to insure that the directions are clearly understood.

### The skills are set up as follows:

COLUMN I — The upper half of Column I requires pictures for single Consonants. The lower half of Column I requires pictures for Digraphs and Blends.

COLUMN II — The upper half of Column II requires words for Short Vowel Families. The lower half of Column II requires words for Sight Families. Have the children <u>line up</u> the words under the Families, as illustrated <u>above</u>.

Long Vowel Families are not included here because they are not as consistent and can be easily misspelled - Ex. rain, rane. Therefore, the Long Vowel Families are reviewed under the next column.

COLUMN III — The Mystery Words on the upper half of Column III are Short or Long Vowel Family words. The Mystery Words on the lower half of Column III are Sight Family words. It may be helpful to bring this fact to the children's attention. These should be decoded as follows:

<u>k</u>ite    What's the family?    ite
        What's the word?       kite

These exercises, from which the children derive great enjoyment, will provide a thorough review of basic decoding skills.

Name: _____

Draw two pictures for each sound.

| c | fl |
|---|---|

Write two words under each family.

| at | ow |
|---|---|
| en | ound |

Draw the Mystery Picture.

top

ball

Name: _____

**Draw two pictures for each sound.**

G _____ | _____

dr _____ | _____

**Write two words under each family.**

ag
___
___

ip
___
___

ar
___
___

ay
___
___

**Draw the Mystery Picture.**

cat

cow

Name: _____

| Draw two pictures for each sound. | Write two words under each family. | | Draw the Mystery Picture. |
|---|---|---|---|
| H _____  cr _____ | __ __ ut<br>__ __ alk | __ __ an<br>__ __ all | p<u>e</u>t<br>h<u>a</u>y |

# Name: _____

| Draw two pictures for each sound. | Write two words under each family. | | Draw the Mystery Picture. |
|---|---|---|---|
| Q _ _ _ _ | ed __ __ | it __ __ | wig |
| cl _ _ _ _ | oo __ __ | ew __ __ | car |

Name: _____

Draw two pictures for each sound. | Write two words under each family. | Draw the Mystery Picture.

| W | ap | un | rake |
| br | oy | oi | chalk |

Name: _____

| Draw two pictures for each sound. | Write two words under each family. | | Draw the Mystery Picture. |
|---|---|---|---|
| y _ _ _ _ | ap __ __ | et __ __ | smile |
| bl _ _ _ _ | ou __ __ | aw __ __ | moon |

Name: _____

| Draw two pictures for each sound. | Write two words under each family. | Draw the Mystery Picture. |
|---|---|---|

**B**

**Ch**

___  ___  in

___  ___  at

**home**

___  ___  er

___  ___  ir

**toy**

**Name:** _____

| Draw two pictures for each sound. | Write two words under each family. | Draw the Mystery Picture. |
|---|---|---|
| D _____ | ug _____  ad _____ | cube |
| Sh _____ | ight _____  igh _____ | saw |

# Name: _____

## Draw two pictures for each sound.

**F**

**Th**

## Write two words under each family.

**eg** ___ ___

**id** ___ ___

**eight** ___ ___

**eigh** ___ ___

## Draw the Mystery Picture.

rain

toy

# Name:

| Draw two pictures for each sound. | Write two words under each family. | | Draw the Mystery Picture. |
|---|---|---|---|
| j | _od_ | _ub_ | feet |
| wh | ought | ange | oil |

Name: _____

Draw two pictures for each sound.

| K | sc |
|---|---|
| _ _ _ | _ _ _ |

Write two words under each family.

| ag | ay |
|---|---|
| __ __ | __ __ |
| __ __ | __ __ |

| ent | oo |
|---|---|
| __ __ | __ __ |
| __ __ | __ __ |

Draw the Mystery Picture.

pie        g<u>ir</u>l

**Name:** _____

| Draw two pictures for each sound. | Write two words under each family. | Draw the Mystery Picture. |
|---|---|---|
| L _____ | ig _____ _____ | soap |
| | ob _____ _____ | |
| pr _____ | ew _____ _____ | fur |
| | ar _____ _____ | |

Name: _____

Draw two pictures for each sound.

| M | pl |
|---|---|

Write two words under each family.

| __ __ ud | __ __ ab |
|---|---|
| __ __ ot | __ __ oin |

Draw the Mystery Picture.

cup

light

**Name:** _____

**Draw two pictures for each sound.**

| N | |
|---|---|
| gr | |

**Write two words under each family.**

| ell | ib |
|---|---|
| ___ ___ | ___ ___ |
| ___ ___ | ___ ___ |

| ow | ound |
|---|---|
| ___ ___ | ___ ___ |
| ___ ___ | ___ ___ |

**Draw the Mystery Picture.**

flag

eight

Name: _____

Draw two pictures for each sound.

| p | gl |
|---|---|

Write two words under each family.

| oss | ight |
|---|---|
| up | igh |

Draw the Mystery Picture.

tent

spoon

# Name:

| Draw two pictures for each sound. | Write two words under each family. | Draw the Mystery Picture. |
|---|---|---|
| R ¦ | **ack**  ___ ___  **eck**  ___ ___ | lips |
| fr ¦ | **alk**  ___ ___  **ur**  ___ ___ | tray |

Name: _____

Draw two pictures for each sound.

S | ch

Write two words under each family.

ick | all

ock | aw

Draw the Mystery Picture.

flame

crowd

# Name: _____

## Draw two pictures for each sound.

| T | _____ |
|---|---|
| sh | _____ |

## Write two words under each family.

| uck | ast |
|---|---|
| ___ ___ | ___ ___ |
| eight | eigh |
| ___ ___ | ___ ___ |

## Draw the Mystery Picture.

| bike |
|---|
| card |

# Name: _____

**Draw two pictures for each sound.**

| V | th |
|---|---|

**Write two words under each family.**

| est | aul |
|---|---|
| ___ ___ | ___ ___ |

| ist | aught |
|---|---|
| ___ ___ | ___ ___ |

**Draw the Mystery Picture.**

r<u>ope</u>    <u>change</u>

Name: _____

| Draw two pictures for each sound. | Write two words under each family. | | Draw the Mystery Picture. |
|---|---|---|---|
| z _____ | ost ___ ___ | ust ___ ___ | whale |
| wh _____ | ought ___ ___ | ange ___ ___ | stew |

# Name:

**Draw two pictures for each sound.**

| c | sp |
|---|---|

**Write two words under each family.**

| and | ar |
|---|---|
| end | alk |

**Draw the Mystery Picture.**

suit

pool

# Name:

## Draw two pictures for each sound.

g

___

sn

___

## Write two words under each family.

| ond | uch |
|---|---|
| ___ | ___ |
| ___ | ___ |

| ound | ight |
|---|---|
| ___ | ___ |
| ___ | ___ |

## Draw the Mystery Picture.

pail

star

Name: _____

Draw two pictures for each sound.

| h | sm |
|---|---|

Write two words under each family.

| ash | ish |
|---|---|
| alk | oy |

Draw the Mystery Picture.

beads
coin

Name: _____

| Draw two pictures for each sound. | Write two words under each family. | Draw the Mystery Picture. |
|---|---|---|
| q ____ | ush ____  ____    ing ____  ____ | tie |
| sl ____ | ew ____  ____    ow ____  ____ | pool |

# Name: _____

## Draw two pictures for each sound.

| w | sk |
|---|----|

## Write two words under each family.

| unch | ight |
|------|------|
| anch | igh  |

## Draw the Mystery Picture.

d o ll

sidewalk

# Name: _____

| Draw two pictures for each sound. | Write two words under each family. | | Draw the Mystery Picture. |
|---|---|---|---|
| y <br><br> _____ | amp <br> _____ <br> _____ | oss <br> _____ <br> _____ | five |
| scr <br><br> _____ | eight <br> _____ <br> _____ | eigh <br> _____ <br> _____ | bar |

92

Name: _____

Draw two pictures for each sound.

| b | Ch |
|---|---|

Write two words under each family.

| ilk | ought |
|---|---|
| ___ | ___ |
| ___ | ___ |

| ept | ange |
|---|---|
| ___ | ___ |
| ___ | ___ |

Draw the Mystery Picture.

toe

paw

# Name: _____

| Draw two pictures for each sound. | Write two words under each family. | Draw the Mystery Picture. |
|---|---|---|
| d <br> ____ | ong <br> ___ <br> ___ | sun |
| | ump <br> ___ <br> ___ | |
| sh <br> ____ | au <br> ___ <br> ___ | bird |
| | aught <br> ___ <br> ___ | |

94

Name: _____

Draw two pictures for each sound.

f _ _ _ _ _

Thr _ _ _ _

Write two words under each family.

ast
___  ___

elt
___  ___

tion
___  ___

sion
___  ___

Draw the Mystery Picture.

h<u>o</u>le

<u>daugh</u>ter

Name: _____

| Draw two pictures for each sound. | Write two words under each family. | Draw the Mystery Picture. |
|---|---|---|
| j _____ | iss ___ ___ | ost ___ ___ | seat |
| Wh _____ | out ___ ___ | oup ___ ___ | straw |

# Name: _____

**Draw two pictures for each sound.**

| k | tw |
|---|----|

**Write two words under each family.**

| _uff | _ound |
|------|-------|
| _ack | _ount |

**Draw the Mystery Picture.**

pl**ant**  j**ar**

Name: _____

| Draw two pictures for each sound. | Write two words under each family. | | Draw the Mystery Picture. |
|---|---|---|---|
| l ____ | est ____ ____ | im ____ ____ | cane |
| tr ____ | ow ____ ____ | er ____ ____ | ground |

98

Name: _____

**Draw two pictures for each sound.**

| sw | m |
|---|---|

**Write two words under each family.**

| ock | oo |
|---|---|
| ___  ___ | ___  ___ |
| ung | oon |
| ___  ___ | ___  ___ |

**Draw the Mystery Picture.**

fr<u>ui</u>t   <u>y</u>ar<u>d</u>

100

# Name: _____

| Draw two pictures for each sound. | Write two words under each family. | | Draw the Mystery Picture. |
|---|---|---|---|
| n _____ | <u>and</u> _____ _____ | <u>eck</u> _____ _____ | b<u>ell</u> |
| str _____ | t<u>o</u> _____ _____ | <u>oi</u>l _____ _____ | cu<u>r</u>l |

# Name: _____

**Draw two pictures for each sound.**

| p | st |
|---|----|
|   |    |

**Write two words under each family.**

| ill | ew |
|-----|-----|
| ___ ___ | ___ ___ |

| and | aw |
|-----|-----|
| ___ ___ | ___ ___ |

**Draw the Mystery Picture.**

Kit<u>e</u>

f<u>light</u>

# Name:

## Draw two pictures for each sound.

r

spr

## Write two words under each family.

um ___  ___

ist ___  ___

ay ___  ___

all ___  ___

## Draw the Mystery Picture.

queen

tool

Name: _____

Draw two pictures for each sound.

| S | ch |
|---|---|
|   |   |

Write two words under each family.

| _end | _ust |
|------|------|
| __irst | __urn |

Draw the Mystery Picture.

milk

spray

**Name:** _____

| Draw two pictures for each sound. | Write two words under each family. | Draw the Mystery Picture. |
|---|---|---|
| t  _____ | **ent** ___ ___ | **ice cream cone** |
| sh _____ | **ick** ___ ___ | |
| | **aul** ___ ___ | **stool** |
| | **aught** ___ ___ | |

# Name: _____

**Draw two pictures for each sound.**

| v | th |
|---|---|

**Write two words under each family.**

| uck | ought |
|---|---|
| ___ ___ | ___ ___ |

| ing | ange |
|---|---|
| ___ ___ | ___ ___ |

**Draw the Mystery Picture.**

c<u>oa</u>t   s<u>leigh</u>

# Name: _____

| Draw two pictures for each sound. | Write two words under each family. | Draw the Mystery Picture. |
|---|---|---|
| z | ill | basket |
|   | ___  ___ |   |
|   | end |   |
|   | ___  ___ |   |
| wh | tion | lightbulb |
|   | ___  ___ |   |
|   | sion |   |
|   | ___  ___ |   |